AF422906

THE OTHER SIDE OF EQUALITY

A Honest Look at Gender, Family and Fairness

MARSHALL JAIRAJ BENJAMIN

The Other Side of Equality
A Honest Look at Gender, Family, and Fairness
© 2025 Marshall Jairaj Benjamin
All rights reserved.

No part of this publication may be reproduced, distributed, or transmitted in any form or by any means, including photocopying, recording, or other electronic or mechanical methods, without the prior written permission of the author, except in the case of brief quotations used in critical reviews and certain other non-commercial uses permitted by copyright law.

For permission requests, Scan the code to connect with Author:

This is a work of non-fiction. All stories, examples, and legal references are based on publicly available information, personal experiences, or those shared with consent. While care has been taken to ensure factual accuracy, the author does not assume responsibility for any outcomes resulting from the use of this information. Readers are advised to consult professionals for legal or psychological matters.

First Edition, 2025
Printed in India

*To every man who stood alone in court,
cried alone in silence,
and fought for fairness in a system that never looked his way.
This book carries your voice.*

Table of Contents

Author's Note

My name is Marshall Jairaj Benjamin. I am a father, a son, a survivor, and now—an author.

I've been called many things: emotional, angry, biased, brave. But I write not to be called anything—I write because silence was killing me.

I've walked through courts where truth didn't matter. I've stood outside locked gates waiting to see my child. I've sat with broken men who didn't want to live another day.
And I've cried behind closed doors because the world didn't believe that men cry too.

This book is not fiction. It is not theory. It is lived reality—mine, and that of millions of others who never got the chance to speak it aloud.

To my son:

If you ever read this, know this was not just a book—it was my heartbeat carved into pages. You are the reason I kept going. And I will wait for you. Always.

Preface

Why This Book Needed to Be Written

I did not set out to become a writer. I set out to become a father, a husband, a provider—someone who could protect his family and live a life of quiet dignity. But somewhere along the way, I found myself standing in a place where none of those identities were allowed to matter. My voice was silenced, my love was questioned, and my existence as a man was reduced to either being useful—or being blamed.

This book was not born from a desire to provoke or polarize. It was born from pain. From nights spent staring at the ceiling, wondering how truth could be so easily ignored. From sitting with broken men—fathers, brothers, sons—whose only crime was trying to fulfill roles society demanded of them. It was born from seeing children grow up without fathers, and fathers grow old without ever hearing their child's voice again.

The word "equality" has been paraded across banners and television screens, celebrated in conferences and campaigns. But what we rarely do is pause and ask: **Equality for whom? At what cost?** And who decides which voices get to be heard?

There is another side to this story—one that doesn't fit the mainstream script. It's a side filled with courtroom battles that never make the news, suicide notes that never get read, and laws that were meant to protect but have turned into tools of silent destruction. It is a side that many are afraid to speak about because it challenges popular belief. But silence is no longer an option. Not for me.

This book is not anti-women. It is not against justice. In fact, it is a plea for justice—for a form of equality that does not exclude half the population to serve the other. It is a reflection, an invitation, and a confrontation. It asks difficult questions—not to divide—but to restore balance where it has been quietly dismantled.

As you turn these pages, you will meet the forgotten. You will hear the voices of those who dared to love, dared to give, and were punished for it. You will walk through broken homes, torn bonds, weaponized laws, and social silence. And perhaps, you will begin to see that true equality cannot be defined by slogans—but only by fairness that touches every human being, not just the favored ones.

This is The Other Side of Equality—and it needed to be written because too many lives have been shattered by a story told only halfway.

Acknowledgments

To every man who dared to speak when the world told him to be quiet—this is your voice.

To the men's rights communities that stood strong even when mocked—thank you for keeping the truth alive.

To the women who stood by men not because of loyalty to gender, but loyalty to justice—your courage is noted.

To the counselors, friends, and strangers who shared their stories with me—you gave this book its spine.

To the laws that failed us—thank you for giving us a reason to fight.

And to the silence... thank you for teaching me how loud the truth can be when it's finally spoken.

Introduction

The Equality We Don't Talk About

You've heard the slogans.
You've read the headlines.
You've watched the marches, the campaigns, the
courtroom victories.

You've heard the word "equality" so many times that it feels
sacred. Unquestionable. Absolute.

And yet, somewhere deep inside—perhaps in a courtroom
corridor, a quiet father's apartment, a boy's tear-stained
pillow—you've sensed that something is off. That what we
call equality doesn't always feel fair. That in trying to
empower one group, we may have forgotten to ask: What
about the other side?

This book isn't about taking sides. It's about **exposing the
imbalance that exists in the name of balance.**

It's about the man who never raised his voice—but lost
everything to an accusation he couldn't defend against.
It's about the father who wakes up every day hoping for a
message from a child he's been legally pushed away from.
It's about the boy who learns, without ever being told
directly, that his feelings are less important, his pain less
visible, and his rights more negotiable.

It's about the quiet deaths—of dignity, of fatherhood, of truth—that occur behind the curtain of progress.

This is not an attack on women. This is not a rejection of feminism in its truest form. It is a demand to re-examine what equality means when it only flows in one direction. It is a call to listen to those we've silenced in our hurry to celebrate empowerment. It is a **journey through the invisible wounds of men**, the overlooked voices of fathers, and the unintended consequences of a movement that forgot to look both ways before marching forward.

In the chapters that follow, you won't just read facts. You'll read grief. Injustice. Stories that didn't make the news. Truths that didn't trend. You'll see how laws meant to protect have been misused. How media manufactures martyrs. How justice, when blinded by gender, becomes something far more dangerous: **selective**.

But more importantly—you'll read hope. The hope that **true equality** is still possible. That we can recalibrate. That fairness is not lost forever—it's just been ignored.

This book is not comfortable.
It is not polite.
But it is necessary.

Welcome to the other side.

Equality or Illusion?

The word "equality" is one of the most powerful in human history. It has brought down empires, built revolutions, and lit fires in the hearts of the oppressed. But like any word used too often without reflection, it has lost its shape. It has been bent, twisted, and—perhaps most dangerously— weaponized.

I grew up believing in equality. I was taught that men and women are equal, and that fairness means treating both with the same respect, dignity, and opportunity. It felt noble, and it felt right. But what I wasn't told—and what most men aren't told—is that the world does not interpret equality the same way for everyone.

Somewhere along the road of progress, equality stopped meaning balance and started meaning favor. Rights became rewards. Protection became privilege. And equality, instead of being a bridge between genders, began to act as a wall—shielding some while suffocating others.

Today, we live in a world where a woman speaking out is seen as brave, but a man speaking out is seen as bitter. A woman's tears are a call to action; a man's tears are a sign of weakness—or worse, guilt. If a woman is hurt, she is a victim. If a man is hurt, he is either invisible or somehow responsible. These are not exaggerations. These are the quiet truths that live beneath the surface of every headline, every courtroom, every family dispute.

The illusion of equality is most evident in the spaces where men are not allowed to be victims. Domestic violence shelters rarely open their doors to abused men. Family courts often assume that the mother is naturally more nurturing. In sexual harassment cases, the presumption of guilt overwhelmingly favors the accuser—if she is a woman. Even the most progressive discussions on gender equality tend to center entirely around the experiences of women, as if men exist only as obstacles to overcome or dangers to survive.

And yet, despite all of this, men continue to stay silent. Why? Because they are told they must be strong. Because they are taught from childhood that their value comes from what they provide, not what they feel. Because admitting to vulnerability is seen as weakness, and weakness is still unforgivable in a man. This silence is not noble—it is deadly.

When laws begin to favor one gender under the guise of protection, when institutions turn a blind eye to the suffering of the other side, and when society paints every man with the brush of suspicion, we are no longer living in a state of equality. We are living in its illusion—a carefully curated image that claims fairness, while quietly practicing bias.

This book is not a rejection of equality. It is a call to return to its original meaning. A reminder that justice cannot be gendered. A warning that any system which elevates one voice by silencing another is not progress—it is oppression wearing a prettier mask.

If we truly want to build a society where men and women stand together, not as competitors but as partners, we must have the courage to confront the imbalance hiding beneath the word "equality." And we must do so not with anger, but with truth.

Because truth—no matter how uncomfortable—is the only thing more powerful than illusion.

The Silence of the Other Side

There is a kind of silence that doesn't come from the absence of words—but from the absence of permission to speak.

For generations, men have been taught to wear armor, not just on battlefields, but in everyday life. Armor made of expectation. Strength without fragility. Sacrifice without complaint. Provision without rest. And above all—silence, even in suffering. Especially in suffering.

It is easy to see women as victims of injustice. Their stories have been told, amplified, and supported by cultural, legal, and institutional frameworks designed to protect them— and rightly so. But where, then, do we place the man who is beaten by his wife? Or the father who is denied access to his child despite court orders? Or the young boy who is molested by a woman and grows up too ashamed to speak of it? Their pain exists—but it has no place. No name. No shelter.

Mainstream narratives have no room for them. The media rarely tells their stories, and when it does, it often treats them as anomalies or worse—mockeries. The man who is slapped in public is laughed at. The father who begs to see his child is seen as desperate, not devoted. The husband who is emotionally tormented is told to "man up" or "take it like a man." These aren't just comments. They are daggers disguised as advice.

And so, men bury their hurt. They don't file complaints—they fear being disbelieved, humiliated, or ridiculed. They don't talk to their friends—because male friendships are rarely built on vulnerability. And they don't seek help—because the world has told them they don't deserve it.

This silence kills. It kills slowly and invisibly. It kills through anxiety attacks hidden under smiles, through depression masked as overworking, through suicides that are dismissed as personal failure rather than societal neglect. When a woman ends her life, people ask what broke her. When a man does, they ask what was wrong with him.

Statistically, men die by suicide at significantly higher rates than women across the world. And yet, this is rarely acknowledged in discussions on mental health. Why? Because acknowledging male vulnerability would require us to admit that the idea of men being inherently stronger, more capable, and emotionally immune is not just wrong—it is dangerous.

This chapter is not about diminishing the struggles women face. It is about demanding recognition that men suffer too—and suffer deeply. And yet, they do so in a world that offers them no stage, no sympathy, and no script to follow.

It's time we stop measuring compassion by gender. A crying man is no less broken than a crying woman. An abused husband is no less wounded than an abused wife. A father longing to hold his child is no less worthy than a mother with the same desire.

The silence of the other side is not empty—it is full of things unsaid, unseen, and unhealed.

And if we truly seek a just society, we must begin by listening to what that silence has always been trying to say.

When Laws Become Weapons

The law is meant to be blind—to status, to race, to gender. It is meant to protect the weak, punish the guilty, and preserve justice. But what happens when the law forgets its neutrality? When protection becomes preference, and justice becomes selective? It stops being a shield—and starts becoming a weapon.

In India and many parts of the world, the legal framework has been shaped—often rightly—to uplift women and protect them from centuries of systemic abuse and suppression. The intentions behind these laws were noble. But intentions mean little when execution becomes imbalance. And in that imbalance, a new kind of victim is born: the innocent man.

Consider the law under IPC Section 498A, created to protect married women from cruelty at the hands of their husbands or in-laws. The law was necessary in a time when such abuse was rampant and often ignored. But over the years, its unchecked application has allowed it to be misused—not by the oppressed, but by the vindictive.

It takes only one complaint—no evidence, no witness, no burden of proof—for a man to be arrested. In many cases, entire families are dragged into FIRs, including elderly parents and even distant relatives. Careers are destroyed.

Reputations shattered. And even if acquitted later, the social death is permanent. The label sticks. The damage is irreversible.

This isn't just theory. I have sat with men who had never stepped inside a police station in their lives, trembling with shame and fear, suddenly being treated like criminals. I have spoken to parents who wept outside courtrooms, unable to comprehend how their lives were upended by a daughter-in-law's false allegation. Not because they were abusive—but because the law allowed her to do it without fear of consequence.

Domestic Violence Acts and maintenance laws often follow a similar arc. They begin as protective tools, but quickly become tactical levers in custody disputes or marital discord. In family courtrooms, the male is rarely given the benefit of doubt. He is seen not as an equal litigant, but as a potential abuser, a presumed liar, a walking ATM.

This legal prejudice is more than injustice—it's institutionalized discrimination. And while false cases are a minority compared to genuine ones, their impact is catastrophic. One false case doesn't just affect one man. It undermines every real victim's credibility and breeds resentment in society.

The system's unwillingness to even acknowledge misuse is where the deepest betrayal lies. Feminist lobbies argue that "even if ten innocent men are punished, it's worth protecting one woman." But what if that innocent man is your son? Your brother? Your father? Justice cannot be built on sacrifice. It must be built on fairness.

Laws that protect one gender by presuming the guilt of another are not laws—they are political instruments. They are tools of social engineering that punish based not on action, but on identity. And when that happens, we are no longer talking about gender justice. We are witnessing legal tyranny.

True equality demands the courage to revisit these laws—not to remove protection from women, but to extend fairness to men. To introduce penalties for false allegations. To ensure that due process is not replaced by public sentiment. To give every accused, regardless of gender, the right to be heard before being condemned.

The court is supposed to be a place of truth. But for many men today, it feels like a graveyard—where their names, reputations, and futures are buried under laws that no longer ask "what happened," but only "who said it."

The time has come to ask—how many more lives must be destroyed before we admit that a law without balance is just another form of injustice?

The Cost of Being a Man

No one is born knowing what it means to be a man. It is not taught in schools. It isn't explained at the dinner table. It is learned through pressure, through silence, through a thousand unspoken expectations placed on the shoulders of boys who are barely old enough to understand the weight.

From the earliest years, boys are nudged toward strength and away from sensitivity. A boy who cries is quickly hushed. A boy who falls is told to get up, not just physically but emotionally. "Be a man," they say—not as encouragement, but as a command. And so, manhood becomes a performance. A role. One that comes with immense cost.

Society expects a man to be a protector, a provider, a problem-solver, and a pillar of strength—no matter the chaos within. He must earn, endure, and provide, often at the expense of his own well-being. He must show up even when he is exhausted, must sacrifice without acknowledgment, and must be okay with the fact that his value is often tied to how much he can offer others.

Marriage, too, is a transaction heavily weighted against him. He is expected to take responsibility for financial stability, while also absorbing emotional damage in silence. If he fails to earn, he is shamed. If he expresses frustration, he is accused of being insensitive. If he walks away, he is irresponsible. And if he stays and suffers, he is invisible.

Work does not spare him either. While society celebrates work-life balance for women, a man juggling multiple jobs to feed his family is seen as doing what is "normal." His burnout is not seen as tragedy—it is seen as duty. No one asks him how he's feeling. No one wonders what he's losing in the process.

Even in emotional spaces, he is denied softness. The phrase "man up" is not a joke—it's a warning. It tells boys and men that their emotions are not welcome, that their pain is a threat to the idea of masculinity. So they suppress it, bury it, deny it—until it eats them from the inside.

The cost of being a man is not just financial—it is spiritual. It is the erosion of identity beneath layers of forced strength. It is isolation disguised as independence. It is fear—of failure, of judgment, of being labeled weak or inadequate. And most dangerously, it is the loss of permission to seek help.

When a man finally breaks, people often ask, "Why didn't he say anything?" The truth is—he was never allowed to. The world never gave him the space. And even if he did speak, would anyone have listened?

I have met countless men who have done everything "right"—worked hard, stayed loyal, carried their families on their backs—and yet found themselves abandoned, blamed, or punished. They didn't ask for much. Just peace. Just fairness. Just a moment to breathe. And yet, that too became a luxury they could not afford.

This chapter is not written to paint men as victims of life—but to acknowledge the unseen taxes they pay simply for being male. It is not about asking for sympathy, but for recognition. Because until we begin to see the emotional, mental, and spiritual toll of forced masculinity, we will keep asking men to carry a weight that eventually breaks them.

And the most tragic part? Most of them won't even cry out as they fall. Because the world has taught them that even their collapse must be quiet.

Raised to Provide, Denied to Feel

How Sons Become Tools and Daughters Become Queens

It starts early—long before school, before law, before society even labels it. It begins in the living room, the kitchen, the whispered praises, and the sharp corrections. It begins in how we love our children differently based on their gender, and what we expect from them in return.

Boys are taught to earn love through performance. "Be strong." "Don't cry." "Take care of your mother." "Protect your sister." These aren't just words—they are codes. Expectations. Silent contracts. And over time, they become the foundation of how a boy sees himself. He learns that to be a good son, a good brother, a good man—he must give. And give quietly.

Meanwhile, girls are often raised with a different narrative. One of protection, emotional validation, celebration. "You are special." "You are a princess." "Your happiness matters." "We'll take care of you." And society delivers on that promise—through culture, media, and even law. Not always, not everywhere, but often enough to create a clear imbalance.

This differential grooming is rarely questioned because it is wrapped in tradition. It is how our parents were raised, and theirs before them. But beneath this generational conditioning lies a harsh truth: **we are raising boys to be tools and girls to be served**. Boys are measured by how much they can suppress. Girls by how much they must be protected.

The result is devastating—not just for men, but for families. The boy who is never allowed to cry grows into a man who doesn't know how to express grief. The son who is told his only worth is in providing becomes a husband who cannot admit when he is broken. And in the end, we call him emotionally unavailable, distant, cold—not realizing we taught him to be that way.

In many families, especially in traditional or patriarchal cultures, daughters are shielded from hardship while sons are thrown into the fire. A daughter fails, she is comforted. A son fails, he is scolded. A daughter is pampered. A son is pressured. And even when love is equal, the form of that love is not. One is soft. The other is steel.

And so, a distorted dynamic emerges. Women grow up expecting care, support, and validation. Men grow up expecting to carry burdens without complaint. When these two meet in adult relationships, conflict is inevitable. The woman expects emotional availability. The man is still decoding what that even means. She wants to be heard. He wants to be safe enough to speak. But his silence is mistaken for apathy, and her expectations are seen as entitlement. No one wins.

Worse still, when family systems enforce this inequality, daughters may grow up with a sense of moral superiority. They are the center of attention, the ones whose emotions matter most. And if this continues unchecked, it breeds entitlement—a belief that sacrifice is a man's job, and happiness a woman's right. A dangerous imbalance that later manifests in one-sided marriages, toxic divorces, and children growing up in fractured homes.

This chapter is not a blame game. It is a mirror—one that forces us to look at how we love, how we raise, and how we unconsciously prepare our children for inequality. If we want sons who are emotionally healthy, we must stop treating them as emotionless soldiers. If we want daughters who respect fairness, we must stop placing them on pedestals that teach them superiority instead of equality.

We must raise our children—not as providers or princesses—but as human beings. With equal rights, equal responsibilities, and equal permission to feel.

Because the cost of failing to do so is not just paid by the child. It is paid by every family, every generation, every broken marriage, every silent father, and every boy who grew up believing that love must be earned through pain.

Marriage: A Risk Without a Safety Net

Marriage, in its purest form, was meant to be a union of two souls—a partnership built on trust, shared values, and unconditional support. For centuries, it was considered sacred, a covenant that survived through storms, sacrifices, and seasons of hardship. But in the modern world, marriage has transformed—not always into a bond of mutual strength, but often into a legal arrangement loaded with risk for one side: the man.

For most men, marriage is not entered lightly. It is a commitment layered with financial responsibilities, emotional investment, and social expectations. He is expected to be the provider, the protector, the patient one, the pillar that holds the structure together—even when it begins to crack.

Yet the moment trouble arises—when disagreements escalate, or misunderstandings evolve into conflict—the ground beneath a man's feet turns dangerously unstable. Suddenly, the very institution he entered in good faith becomes a minefield. Because while marriage laws claim to protect both spouses, in practice, they offer far more security to one than the other.

In many countries, particularly in India, once a marriage breaks down, the law becomes an uneven battlefield. A woman can file cases under IPC 498A for cruelty, even without substantial evidence. She can demand maintenance regardless of her capacity to earn. She can initiate Domestic Violence cases, move out with the child, and block access, and the man is expected to prove his innocence while carrying the weight of suspicion.

And the system seldom stops to ask: What if the man is innocent?
There are no support centers for emotionally abused husbands. No shelters for fathers thrown out of their homes. No legal presumption that he might be the victim, not the aggressor. His assets may be frozen, his home taken, his job affected by the strain of court appearances, and his social circle fractured by whispers and judgment.

What makes this even more brutal is the silence surrounding it. Society, media, and even extended families often refuse to acknowledge that men can suffer in marriages—not just from physical abuse, but from emotional manipulation, threats, humiliation, and constant devaluation. They are told to "adjust," "be patient," "stay for the child," or worst of all, "this is how women are—tolerate it."

And so, many men stay—not out of love, but out of fear. Fear of false cases. Fear of losing access to their children. Fear of being portrayed as the villain. Fear of the system, not just the spouse. Marriage for them becomes less of a relationship and more of a contract with unbalanced clauses.

What's tragic is that most of these men did not fail at love. They failed at protecting themselves from a system that punishes them for being male. They entered the bond with hope, and often, with deep affection. They supported their wives' ambitions, fulfilled family duties, and sacrificed personal dreams. Yet, when the foundation shook, they discovered there was no safety net beneath them. No presumption of fairness. No one who would hear their side.

This is not to suggest that women do not face real suffering in marriage. They do, and many have endured great injustices. But the conversation has become so lopsided that to speak of male suffering is seen as a threat to progress. And this silence, once again, becomes the accomplice of injustice.

A healthy society cannot function on a legal system that offers protection to one partner and punishment to the other based on gender alone. True marital harmony cannot exist when one party is legally invincible, and the other is permanently at risk.

Marriage must return to its original form: a partnership of equality—not just in duties, but in dignity and rights. Until then, for many men, getting married will continue to feel like climbing a mountain blindfolded—with no rope, no harness, and no assurance that the law will catch them if they fall.

And far too many are falling.

Custody Battles and the Death of Fatherhood

There are losses that are physical—measurable, visible, finite. And then there are losses that leave no scars on the skin but tear something far deeper: the bond between a father and his child. Few things destroy a man more quietly, more completely, than being told that his role as a father is negotiable... or worse, unnecessary.

In the eyes of the law, a child is often seen not as a soul with two parents, but as property to be "awarded," "granted," or "allowed." And when a marriage ends, the legal system—especially in many traditional societies—assumes the child belongs with the mother. Not because of a case-specific psychological assessment. Not because of proven facts. But simply because she is the mother.

In most custody battles, fathers are reduced to "visitors." Weekends. Alternate holidays. A few hours under supervision, or worse, digital calls that are often ignored, blocked, or sabotaged. The court says he has visitation rights. But who enforces them when they're violated? Who ensures that the child is not being alienated, manipulated, or slowly turned against him?

I have seen fathers travel miles every weekend, only to wait at locked doors. I've seen them buy birthday gifts they never get to give. I've read messages left unread, heard their voices break mid-sentence while recalling a child's first word or last hug. And I have seen the hollow that grows in a man's chest when his child stops recognizing him—not because he abandoned the child, but because the system forced him into absence.

For these men, fatherhood becomes a ghost. They exist as names on birth certificates, as bank transfers for school fees and maintenance, as old photographs that fade while someone else writes the child's story. And yet, they're expected to remain calm. To obey the system. To wait.

The law claims to act "in the best interest of the child." But what greater interest could there be than preserving the bond with both parents—unless one is proven harmful? A loving father is not a visitor. He is not an accessory. He is not an option. He is essential.

And yet, our legal structure has failed to evolve with this truth. There is no shared parenting law. No effective enforcement of visitation. No consequences for parental alienation unless it turns into something extreme. The assumption that "mothers are naturally better caregivers" is treated like gospel, despite countless studies showing that children thrive best when both parents are involved, emotionally and consistently.

What's worse is the emotional isolation. Fathers who speak up about custody pain are often met with indifference— even from their own families. "Let it go," they are told. "The child will understand when they grow up." But years pass. Birthdays are missed. Milestones become memories he only hears about, never witnesses. And by the time the child is old enough to "understand," the distance has done its damage.

It is not just the father who suffers. The child does too. A part of their emotional structure—the balance of love, discipline, identity—is compromised. They grow up with half the picture. And too often, with half-truths. In a society that constantly champions mothers, the absence of a father is rarely questioned. But its consequences are profound.

This chapter is not written in anger. It is written in mourning. For the fathers who tried. For the children who wondered why their dad disappeared. And for the justice system that still fails to recognize that taking a child away from a loving parent is not just legal bias—it is emotional cruelty.

If we claim to care about family, we must care about fathers. Not just in biology, but in presence, in voice, in right. Because when we deny children their fathers, we are not only killing fatherhood.

We are killing futures.

The Mother is Always Right – And Other Myths

There is no denying the sanctity of motherhood. A mother brings life into the world, nurtures it with her body, and often sacrifices much for her children. But somewhere along the line, the sacredness of motherhood became something else—a shield of unquestionable moral authority. Society began to believe not just that mothers are important, but that mothers are always right.

This belief is so deeply rooted that it seeps into every institution—homes, schools, media, and most critically, the judicial system. When disputes arise, when custody battles unfold, when conflict turns into courtroom warfare, the mother is often presumed to be the more capable, more innocent, more trustworthy parent. Not because evidence proves it, but because the narrative demands it.

But motherhood, like fatherhood, is a human role. And human beings are complex. Capable of love, yes—but also of manipulation, bitterness, control, and even cruelty. The idea that all mothers are automatically good, nurturing, and selfless is not just false—it is dangerous.

I have met mothers who have alienated their children from the father out of revenge, not protection. I have seen mothers weaponize their love—using it to guilt, to manipulate, to create dependency. I've seen them refuse to comply with visitation orders, coaching children to fear or hate the father. And the system, blinded by this myth, stands still—unwilling to believe that a mother can be wrong.

The damage caused by this blind faith isn't only to the father—it is deeply etched into the child's psyche. When a mother lies, the child absorbs confusion as truth. When a mother vilifies, the child grows up with inherited hatred. When a mother blocks love from the other parent, the child's heart is taught to function with one valve closed.

And yet, even when fathers raise their voices, they are met with judgment. "Don't speak against the mother of your child." "Don't dishonor the woman who gave birth." "Take the high road." But what is the high road when your child is being slowly pulled away from you by manipulation disguised as motherhood? What is dignity worth if your silence becomes the rope that strangles your fatherhood?

This myth of maternal perfection also harms mothers themselves. It places an inhuman expectation on them—to be infallible, endlessly giving, and morally superior at all times. It denies them space to fail, to be flawed, or to seek help. In truth, no parent is always right. Not mother, not father. We are all trying, failing, growing.

But only one side is allowed the grace of failure.

The truth is uncomfortable, but it must be told: Not every mother is a nurturer. Not every mother is motivated by the child's best interest. And not every father who raises his voice is bitter or vengeful. Sometimes, he's just trying to save his child from emotional harm that wears a maternal mask.

We must move beyond these myths. Justice cannot be built on romanticized roles. If we truly believe in the well-being of children, we must assess each parent not by their gender, but by their actions, their capacity to love, their willingness to cooperate, and their psychological stability.

It's time we tell the truth with maturity and fairness.

Mothers are not always right.
Fathers are not always wrong.
And children deserve more than a narrative. They deserve the truth.

Parental Alienation – The Emotional Genocide

Not all abuse leaves bruises. Some leaves silence. Some leaves distance. Some turns a child's heart into a battlefield—where love is slowly replaced by doubt, loyalty becomes fear, and one parent becomes the enemy in a story they never got to tell.

Parental alienation is not a term that finds space in popular conversations. It doesn't trend on hashtags. It doesn't receive sympathy from talk shows or awareness campaigns. But it is real. It is devastating. And it is happening all around us—in homes that look normal from the outside but are quietly collapsing from within.

At its core, parental alienation is the systematic manipulation of a child's mind to turn them against one parent—usually after a separation or divorce. The alienating parent, often the one with physical custody, creates an environment where the child is emotionally, and sometimes psychologically, programmed to reject the other parent. Not based on abuse. Not based on neglect. But based on the alienator's own hatred, control, or vindictiveness.

The tools of alienation are subtle. It begins with withholding communication. Then comes bad-mouthing. Planting seeds of fear: "Your father doesn't love you," or "He left us because you weren't important." Sometimes, it's guilt: "If you love him, it means you don't love me." Other times, it's forced loyalty: "You're not allowed to talk to him."

And the child, torn between love and fear, begins to pull away—not out of choice, but survival. The bond they once shared with their father erodes. The voice that once comforted them becomes strange. The visits feel awkward. The phone calls become rare. And eventually, silence becomes normal.

To the outside world, it looks like the child simply doesn't want to see the other parent. But inside, that child is caught in a psychological tug-of-war. One they never signed up for. One they are too young to understand.

What makes this even more heartbreaking is that the very institutions meant to protect children have failed to even acknowledge the trauma. In 2019, the Supreme Court of India rejected the concept of parental alienation, refusing to recognize it as a form of psychological harm or mental cruelty to children. This wasn't just a judicial oversight—it was a loud message that the emotional suffering of children separated from a loving parent is not worthy of legal concern.

This decision didn't just undermine the experiences of thousands of alienated fathers. It effectively told the alienating parent that emotional manipulation was not abuse—as long as it didn't leave physical wounds. It left countless children unprotected, and countless fathers powerless, while reinforcing the dangerous idea that a child's resistance to seeing one parent must always be legitimate, never influenced.

And the alienated parent? He watches in agony.
He sees the child's face grow colder.

He hears their voice lose warmth.
He reads their messages—if they come at all—and senses the distance stretching wider, day by day.

He wants to scream, to fight, to hold his child and explain. But courts move slowly. Society stays indifferent. And if he raises his voice too loud, he's told to back off, to "give space," to "not traumatize the child." No one sees that the trauma is already happening. That the real abuser is not the one being erased, but the one doing the erasing.

Parental alienation is child abuse—camouflaged as custody. It doesn't just steal years. It steals trust, identity, connection, and sometimes, the child's own sense of self. Because every child is half of each parent. To turn them against one half is to teach them to hate a part of themselves.

The damage doesn't end in childhood. Alienated children often grow up with unresolved emotional pain. Some later discover the truth, and are consumed with guilt for the years lost. Others never reconnect. Some spiral into addiction, aggression, or mental health struggles—unable to name what broke inside them. And many alienated fathers die waiting for a reunion that never comes.

What makes this genocide emotional is that it doesn't kill the body—it kills the bond. It kills memory. It kills the sacred connection that a parent and child are meant to share. And it does so with surgical precision, sanctioned by silence, and often protected by the very institutions meant to preserve family.

This chapter is not just a warning. It is a plea.
To parents: Do not poison your child to punish your partner.
To courts: Recognize the psychological abuse that alienation causes.
To society: Stop treating fatherhood as optional.
And to the child—if you are reading this as a grown adult, know this: your father may have never stopped loving you. He just ran out of ways to reach you.

Parental alienation may not leave blood on the floor. But it leaves graves in the heart.

And the worst part? No one even mourns them.

Fake Feminism and the Industry of Victimhood

There was a time when feminism was a beacon of justice. When it marched through the streets demanding the right to vote, the right to study, the right to work, and the right to be safe. It was noble. It was needed. And it was built on the courage of women who had been denied their humanity for too long.

But somewhere along the way, something changed. The movement that once fought for equality began seeking advantage. The call for fairness was slowly replaced by a hunger for supremacy. Feminism, once about rights, became about narratives. About who could speak. Who could accuse. Who could never be questioned.

And thus was born fake feminism—a mutated version of the original vision. One that feeds on victimhood, punishes dissent, and silences anyone who dares to say: What about the men?

In this version, women are always oppressed, always right, always innocent. Men, by contrast, are always privileged, always suspect, always guilty. It doesn't matter what the facts are. It doesn't matter who is hurt. What matters is control—over the narrative, the law, the media, and increasingly, the truth itself.

Fake feminism has mastered the art of selective empathy. A woman breaks down—she is a survivor. A man breaks down—he is unstable or manipulative. A woman files a

complaint—it is taken at face value. A man does the same—
he is questioned, mocked, or ignored. It is not equality. It is
entitlement masked as empowerment.

Entire industries now thrive on this narrative. Corporates
promote "diversity" by sidelining qualified men. Media
channels run stories without verifying facts—because if a
woman claims abuse, it must be true. NGOs receive crores
in funding to fight "gender-based violence," while never
acknowledging the violence inflicted on men. Legal
systems introduce gender-specific protections, but no
mechanisms to hold false accusers accountable.

And behind all this, an economy of outrage flourishes.
News anchors sell victimhood. Politicians cash in on
emotional optics. Social media influencers build careers off
curated trauma. Pain becomes a product, and feminism
becomes a brand. The cause, once rooted in balance, is now
a machine—manufacturing fear, guilt, and compliance.

But perhaps the greatest betrayal of all is this: real women's
issues are now buried beneath false ones. When fake cases
dominate headlines, true victims are doubted. When
empowered women misuse laws, the ones still fighting for
genuine equality lose credibility. And when feminism
becomes a shield for unchecked behavior, it fails both
women and men alike.

This is not a rejection of feminism—it is a rejection of its
hijacking.
Of the silence around false accusations.
Of the immunity granted to manipulation.
Of the demonization of masculinity as a default threat.

The truth is, we cannot build a just world by swinging the pendulum too far to either side. Men and women are not enemies. And victimhood is not a gender—it is a human condition.

Fake feminism thrives on division. It survives by silencing dissent. But truth... truth has a longer life.

And the truth is: justice must serve the facts—not the favored.

If we want a future where women are empowered and men are respected, we must first dismantle the industry of victimhood and return to the essence of equality—not just in law, but in heart.

Because the cause is too important to be corrupted. And too many lives have already paid the price.

Media, Money, and Manufactured Martyrs

Truth is no longer what happened. It is what gets the most views.

In the age of noise, media doesn't tell stories—it sells them. Pain is packaged. Outrage is edited. Victimhood is scripted to fit a narrative that guarantees engagement. And within this spectacle, the suffering of men becomes inconvenient. Unmarketable. Unwelcome.

When a woman cries on television, there is background music, cutaway shots, hashtags ready to trend. But when a man cries, the camera rarely stays. His pain doesn't translate well into a headline. It doesn't provoke the right kind of outrage. It doesn't fit the storyline that the media has spent decades refining: that men are the problem, and women are always the wounded.

This isn't to say that women's stories don't deserve attention—they do. But when media deliberately filters pain through gender, what we get is not information. It is indoctrination.

In countless cases, men have been named, shamed, and vilified before a single hearing in court. Their faces splashed across news channels, their careers destroyed in real-time, their families left to deal with the fallout. And yet, when those same men are proven innocent, the silence from the media is deafening. There are no follow-up reports. No apologies. No attempt to restore the dignity that was publicly stolen.

Because there's no money in vindication. But there's a fortune in accusation.

And behind the cameras, the business model is clear: sell the emotion, not the evidence. Fundraisers surge when the victim is a woman. NGO donations rise. Grants are awarded. Awards are handed out. Corporates push their CSR campaigns in the name of "gender empowerment," even if the reality is far more nuanced.

A single viral case can become a career launchpad for activists, influencers, and even political campaigns. The "survivor" is placed on panels, interviewed endlessly, quoted in articles—and whether the case was true or not, becomes irrelevant. The image has already been built. The martyr has already been manufactured.

Meanwhile, men's issues—mental health, suicides, false accusations, custody alienation—are rarely mentioned. And when they are, they're framed with suspicion, softened with disclaimers, or buried under the obligation to mention "women suffer more." As if pain must compete. As if justice must be rationed.

Even entertainment is not spared. Movies glorify female revenge without context. Web series show men as predators by default. Sitcoms laugh at abusive wives, joke about fathers being clueless, and normalize the humiliation of men. Slowly, subtly, the public is taught that male suffering is either deserved—or laughable.

This machinery—of media, money, and selective storytelling—has not just skewed perception. It has institutionalized bias. It has built a world where truth must pass through the filter of gender before it is believed.

And in this world, men don't just lose their rights. They lose their stories.

This chapter is not an attack on journalism. It is a call to integrity. A plea that truth must be sacred, not sponsored. That victims come in all genders, and justice begins with listening—not labeling.

Because when the media chooses sides instead of facts, and when pain is monetized instead of understood, we no longer live in an informed society.

We live in a manipulated one.

And in such a world, every broken man who dies unheard adds another silence to the growing graveyard of truths we chose not to tell.

Men's Rights Is Not Misogyny

Say the words "men's rights" out loud and watch the reactions change. Eyes narrow. Smirks surface. Accusations come flying. Misogynist. Woman-hater. Chauvinist. The labels arrive faster than any effort to understand.

It is one of the greatest ironies of modern discourse: the very movement that dares to speak about equality for men is dismissed as a threat to equality itself.

Let's be clear—men's rights activism is not about hating women. It's about refusing to be hated simply for being men.

It is not against women's progress. It is against the idea that men must regress for women to rise. It is not about rolling back rights. It is about ensuring that rights do not become privileges cloaked in victimhood, handed out to one gender while the other is stripped of even basic fairness.

Men's rights activism was born not in rebellion, but in necessity. It rose from courtrooms where innocent men were dragged through years of false cases. From funeral pyres of fathers who died by suicide after being denied access to their children. From shelters that turned away male victims of domestic violence. From HR departments where men were guilty until proven innocent. From the silence that buried every story that didn't fit the feminist script.

MRAs didn't ask for a war. They asked for a conversation. They asked for data, dialogue, and dignity. And in return, they were laughed at, labeled toxic, or ignored entirely.

But make no mistake—this movement is not going away. It is growing. Quietly. Relentlessly. Not with slogans, but with truths too bitter to be denied any longer.

It is fueled not by hate, but by heartbreak.
By fathers sitting outside family courts, clinging to photos of children they're not allowed to meet.
By husbands thrown into jails on the basis of words, not evidence.
By sons who were taught to protect everyone but were protected by no one.
By men who were never told they had the right to cry, let alone the right to justice.

Still, society insists: "But men already have everything." As if economic participation erases emotional pain. As if being less likely to be raped makes it acceptable to be falsely accused. As if having more CEOs justifies having more suicides.

Men's rights activism doesn't deny the struggles women face. It simply refuses to pretend that men don't struggle at all.

It demands shared parenting not because mothers are bad— but because fathers matter too.

It calls out false accusations not to protect predators—but to protect the wrongly punished.

It asks for mental health support not because men are weak—but because strength should not mean silence.

And it stands against laws that judge by gender instead of evidence, not because it wants women vulnerable—but because it wants justice to mean something again.

What men's rights activism truly asks is this: Why should one gender's pain be the price for another's empowerment?

The movement is not misogyny.
It is a resistance to misandry.
It is a refusal to be the invisible collateral damage of a one-sided revolution.
And it is a reminder that true equality includes everyone—even the ones no one wants to hear.

If standing up for men who are wrongfully accused, silenced, or destroyed by systemic bias makes one an MRA, then wear the title with pride.

Because this world doesn't need fewer men speaking.

It needs more people listening.

Restoring Balance

Equality is not a war. It is not a game of who suffers more, or who shouts louder. It is a balancing act—one that demands maturity, not militancy. And yet, for far too long, the scales have tilted under the weight of selective empathy and politicized pain.

The cost of this imbalance is clear. Men have been buried beneath presumption. Women have been used as political pawns. Children have been reduced to leverage in custody battles. Families have been destroyed—not by love lost, but by laws misused. And still, society clings to slogans that sound noble but ring hollow when tested in real life.

It is time to stop shouting and start listening. To step away from extremism on both ends and move toward restoration—not retribution.

But what does that look like?

First, we must rewrite the laws that have become weapons. Gender-specific provisions that presume guilt based on identity have no place in a democratic society. False accusations must carry consequences—not because we wish to scare victims away, but because we must protect truth. The moment we allow lies to roam freely under the shelter of "protection," we undermine justice itself.

Second, we need shared parenting laws. A child is not property to be won. A child is love, memory, connection—and that requires both parents. Unless there is proven harm, no parent should be removed from a child's life.

Family courts must stop operating under outdated assumptions that only mothers can nurture. Fathers are not visitors. They are not replacements. They are essential.

Third, there must be support structures for male victims—of domestic violence, emotional abuse, and parental alienation. Just as women have crisis centers, helplines, and shelters, men deserve spaces where their pain is acknowledged without ridicule or reversal of blame.

Fourth, mental health must become gender-inclusive. Suicide prevention cannot ignore the demographic that constitutes the majority of deaths by suicide—men. We must dismantle the myth that strength means silence, and begin normalizing male vulnerability—not in theory, but in actual policy and outreach.

Fifth, gender studies and social narratives must evolve. Feminism, in its original form, had merit. But today, we need balance. Gender studies programs must include men's issues—not as footnotes, but as primary concerns. Media must begin telling both sides. Schools must teach compassion, not division.

And finally, we need to retrain the collective moral compass. Men are not disposable. Women are not flawless. Children are not weapons. Pain has no gender. And justice must begin with the courage to see reality as it is—not as it's been sold to us.

Restoring balance does not mean diminishing women. It means recognizing that empowering one group should never require erasing another.

We are not enemies. We are halves of a whole.
And if we keep fighting for dominance instead of
understanding, we will raise generations that inherit our
wounds—not our wisdom.

This is not about revenge. This is about recalibration.
And it starts with truth.
It starts with accountability.
It starts with listening to the voices we were taught to
ignore.

Because balance is not just a principle of justice. It is a
foundation of peace.

And peace is long overdue.

A Child's Right to Both Parents

In every custody battle, beneath the court files, beneath the legal jargon and affidavits, there lies a child. Not a pawn. Not a possession. A living, breathing soul—caught in a storm they never created.

We talk a lot about parents' rights. About who gets the child, who pays maintenance, who has visitation. But what is almost never asked is: what does the child need? What does the child deserve?

And the answer, almost always, is this: a child deserves both parents—in love, in presence, in influence, and in memory.

The bond between a parent and a child is not interchangeable. No father can replace a mother's touch. No mother can replace a father's presence. They are different, not in value, but in essence. Together, they create emotional balance. Without one, that balance is fractured.

Yet our family courts, our cultural assumptions, and our legal frameworks often treat fathers as optional. In custody disputes, the child is routinely placed with the mother by default—unless extreme evidence shows otherwise. Fathers are offered "visitation," as if their role is that of an outsider, a guest, a second-tier participant in their own child's life.

But ask any child who has been alienated from a loving parent—and they will tell you: something is missing. And that absence echoes across their emotional development, their trust in relationships, their self-worth, and sometimes, their very identity.

Children are observant. They pick up not just on what is said, but what is denied. When they see one parent demonized, blocked, or erased, they internalize that narrative. And often, they grow up confused—believing half of themselves is bad, wrong, or unworthy.

This emotional disfigurement doesn't fade with age. It calcifies. It turns into rebellion, depression, anxiety, aggression, or detachment. And by the time they realize what they've lost, the bond has already withered—too much time, too many lies, too much silence.

We must remember: a child's heart doesn't understand courtroom logic. It doesn't care who filed first or who won custody. What it understands is love. Presence. Truth. And when one parent is absent—not by choice, but by force— that child suffers a wound that no legal order can heal.

Shared parenting isn't just a legal necessity—it's an emotional imperative. Unless proven unfit or dangerous, both parents should remain active, involved, and present in the child's life. Not as competitors, but as co-guardians of that child's emotional future.

This is not about splitting time with mathematical precision. It's about preserving connection. It's about birthday calls that aren't filtered through court orders. It's about school events attended by both parents. It's about allowing the child to form their own bond, their own memories, their own understanding of love—free from manipulation.

And when parents fail to honor that? When they weaponize children to hurt each other? That isn't just cruelty to the other parent. That is child abuse. Subtle. Sanctioned. But abuse nonetheless.

We need laws that recognize a child's right to both parents—not just in principle, but in enforcement. We need educational systems that acknowledge the importance of fatherhood. We need media that stops portraying single motherhood as heroic by default, and instead begins promoting cooperative co-parenting as the ideal.

Most importantly, we need a cultural shift—one that understands that no court, no lawyer, and no grudge has the right to amputate a parent from a child's heart.

Because in the end, children don't care about who was "right."
They care about who was there.

And if we continue to normalize their separation from loving fathers, we're not protecting children.

We are failing them—permanently.

Beyond Labels – The Human Rights Approach

At some point, every fight for justice must ask a deeper question:
Are we still fighting for humanity—or are we just fighting each other?

In the endless battle of labels—feminist vs. MRA, victim vs. accused, man vs. woman—we've lost sight of something fundamental: we are all human first.

We bleed.
We break.
We love.
We fear.
And we suffer.

Pain doesn't come color-coded by gender.
Suffering doesn't choose its victims based on chromosomes.

But our systems, our laws, our media, and even our moral compasses have been structured to divide compassion. They tell us that some pain matters more than others. That some stories deserve a microphone, while others must settle for silence.

This binary thinking is not progress. It is prejudice in a new disguise.

True justice cannot be gendered.
True fairness cannot be one-sided.
And equality must mean equal concern—not selective outrage.

The future we must strive for is not one where women dominate or men reclaim. It is a world where both are safe, both are heard, and both are held accountable when wrong.

We must start talking about human rights, not gender battles.

A father's right to raise his child is not a male right—it's a human right.
A man's right to defend himself against false accusations is not male privilege—it's basic justice.
A boy's right to cry, to seek mental health care, to be free from gender expectations—these aren't fringe issues. They are core human needs.

And yes, a woman's right to safety, opportunity, and respect is non-negotiable—but so is a man's.

We do not have to diminish one to uplift the other.

The human rights approach means moving beyond activism built on gender warfare. It means rejecting victimhood as currency. It means that truth matters more than identity.

When someone is abused, the question must not be: "Is it a woman?"
It must be: "What happened?"
When someone lies, the question must not be: "Do we

believe them anyway?"
It must be: "Can the truth survive scrutiny?"

In courts. In homes. In society.
We need to build systems that prioritize evidence, not emotion.
That recognize the human being behind the story—not the stereotype in front of it.

Because at the end of it all, beneath the legal arguments and ideological noise, we're all looking for the same thing:
To be heard.
To be seen.
To be treated fairly.

Human rights are not about which gender gets more. They are about ensuring no one gets less—just because of who they are.

It is time we lay down the swords of gender politics. It is time we walk together—not in competition, but in conviction.
Because the future will not be shaped by feminists or MRAs alone.

It will be shaped by those brave enough to put humanity first.

The Other Side of Equality

We began with a word—equality—a word so powerful it has launched revolutions, redefined rights, and shaped the direction of nations. But like all powerful words, when misunderstood, it can cause quiet devastation.

This book has not been a denial of equality. It has been a mirror—held up to the side no one wants to look at. The other side. The inconvenient side. The side that has been buried under movements, hashtags, policy drafts, and political correctness.

On one side of equality, we see empowerment. On the other, silence.
On one side, protection. On the other, presumption of guilt.
On one side, support structures, social campaigns, legal shields. On the other, men trying to prove they're human before they're judged.

Equality, as it exists today, is not equal. It is a painting with half the canvas colored, and the rest left blank—dismissed, denied, or distorted.

Men have been told they're privileged. That they hold all the cards. But what good are those cards when your rights are torn apart in a courtroom based on assumptions? What is privilege when your cries are met with laughter, your innocence with indifference, your pain with suspicion?

We've raised boys to protect, and then blamed them for being emotionally distant.
We've raised men to provide, and then labeled them toxic for failing to emote on command.
We've asked them to be strong, silent, reliable, and replaceable—and when they break, we act surprised.

The other side of equality is not about asking for more. It is about asking for fairness.
It is not anti-woman. It is pro-truth.
It is not a denial of history. It is a demand that history no longer be used to justify present injustice.

What we seek is not to roll back progress for women—it is to extend that progress to include men.

To say that both can suffer.
Both can harm.
Both can heal.
And both deserve protection when they're victims, accountability when they're guilty, and dignity at all times—regardless of gender.

This is the equality we were promised.
Not a battlefield of blame, but a common ground of mutual respect.

This book was written not because I have all the answers, but because I could no longer live with the silence. Because I have seen too many men die with their truth buried under shame. Because I have met too many children growing up fatherless, not because their fathers didn't love them—but because someone decided that love didn't matter.

The other side of equality is real.
It is filled with broken families, criminalized fathers,
silenced boys, and forgotten truths.
But it is also filled with people who are beginning to speak.
People like you—who chose to read this, question what
you were taught, and open your heart to a reality that lives
quietly in the shadows.

And maybe, just maybe, if we can learn to see both sides,
we can finally build a world that doesn't need books like
this anymore.

Until then—this truth stands.

Unapologetic.
Uncompromised.
And undivided.

Afterword

Truth Echoes Longer Than Noise

This book was not easy to write. Not because the words were hard to find—but because the truths behind them were heavy to carry. Every chapter came from stories lived, losses witnessed, and voices ignored for far too long.

I don't expect everyone to agree with this book. That was never the goal. But I do hope—if nothing else—that it made you pause. That it made you think. That it made you look at pain differently—not as a competition between genders, but as a shared human burden.

I hope it made space in your heart for the men you once dismissed.
The father you thought didn't try hard enough.
The friend who stopped speaking after his divorce.
The boy who laughed too much, and died too young.
The man who looked fine, until he wasn't.

This isn't just a book. It's a conversation that should've started years ago.

If you've made it this far, thank you.
For your time.
For your willingness to listen.
For being part of the change.

We may never undo all the damage that's been done.
But together, we can stop adding to it.

Other books by the Author

The Silent Genocide

India's Male Suicide Epidemic and the Erosion of Human Rights

In this groundbreaking work, Marshall Jairaj Benjamin unveils the harrowing truth behind India's alarming male suicide rates—exposing how social neglect, legal bias, and emotional isolation have created a silent epidemic. Through deeply researched insights, real-life stories, and emotional storytelling, The Silent Genocide challenges us to rethink mental health, gender justice, and human rights from the side that's rarely spoken about.

Available on:
📖 Amazon | 📖 Notion Press | 📖 Flipkart

Join Author's Whatsapp Channel for updates, Scan the code:

www.ingramcontent.com/pod-product-compliance
Lightning Source LLC
Chambersburg PA
CBHW040828120726

48005CB00012B/1539